HUMAN BODY BOOK

INTRODUCTION TO THE NERVOUS SYSTEM

Children's Anatomy & Physiology Edition

Speedy Publishing LLC
40 E. Main St. #1156
Newark, DE 19711
www.speedypublishing.com

The nervous system
is a control system
of the body and is a
bit like a computer.

The nervous system is
the highway along which
your brain sends and
receives information
about what is happening
in the body and around it.

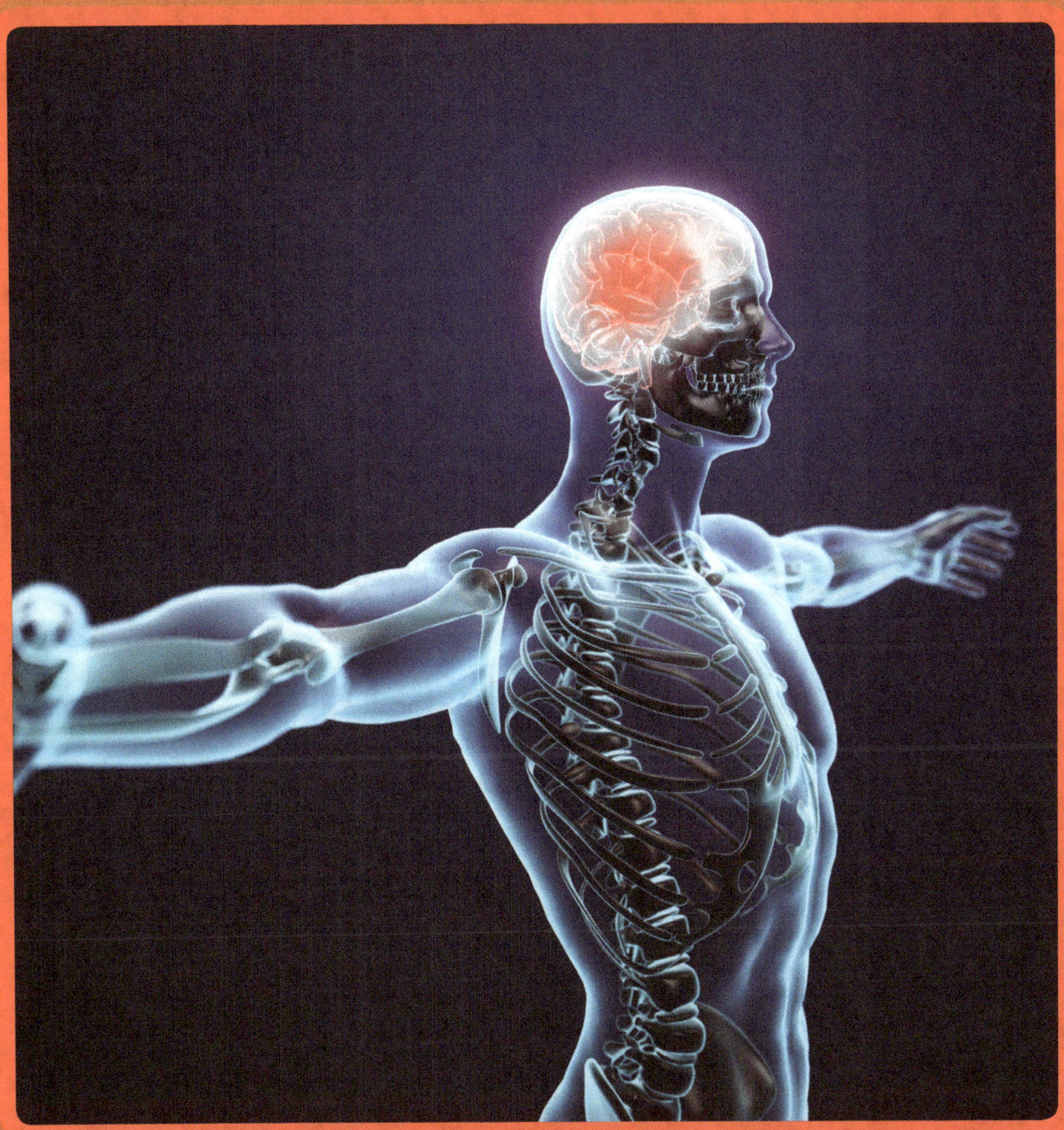

This highway is made
up of billions of nerve
cells, or neurons
which join together
to make nerves.

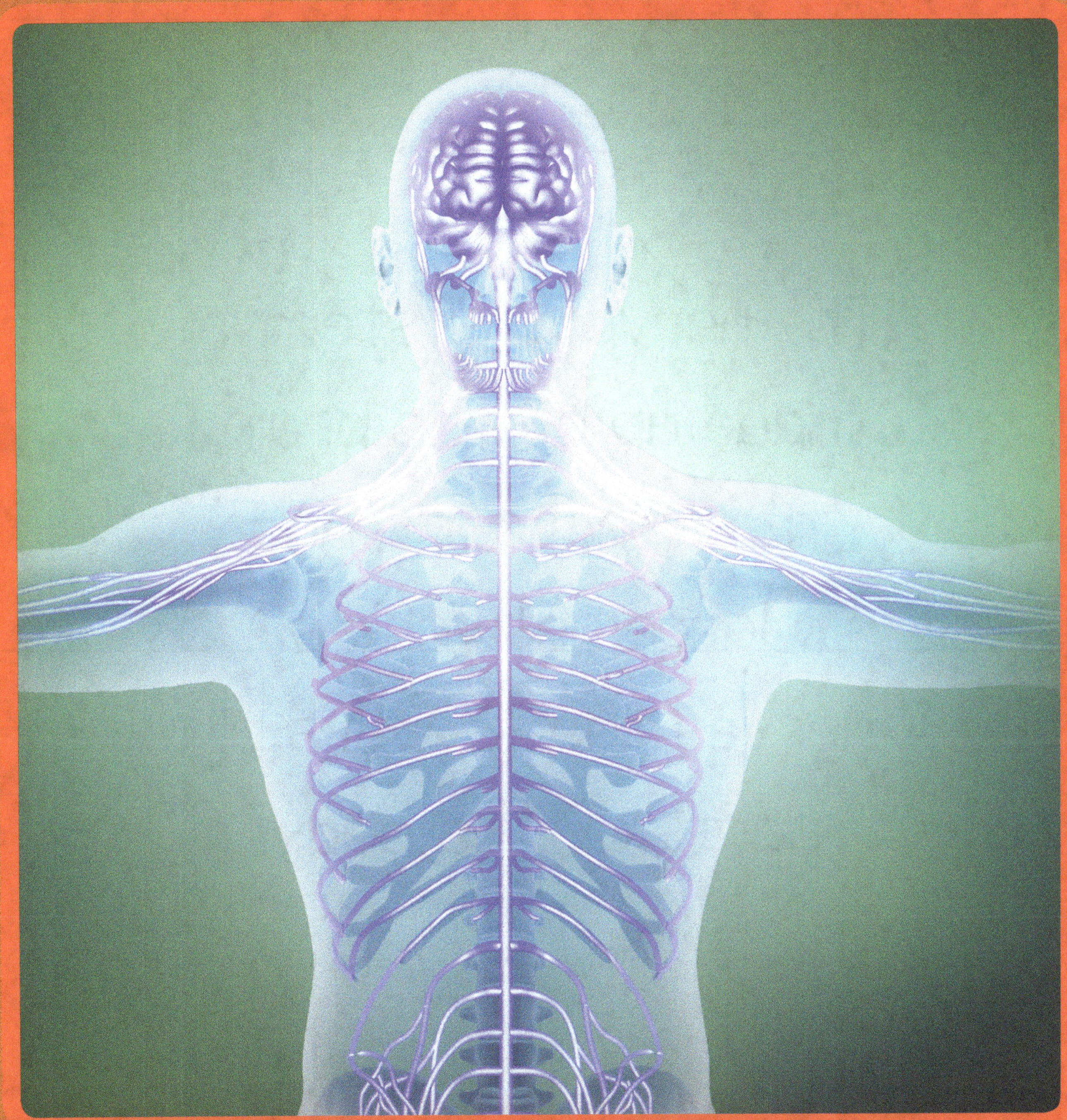

The nervous system is
made up of the brain,
the spinal cord, and
a large network of
nerves that covers all
parts of the body.

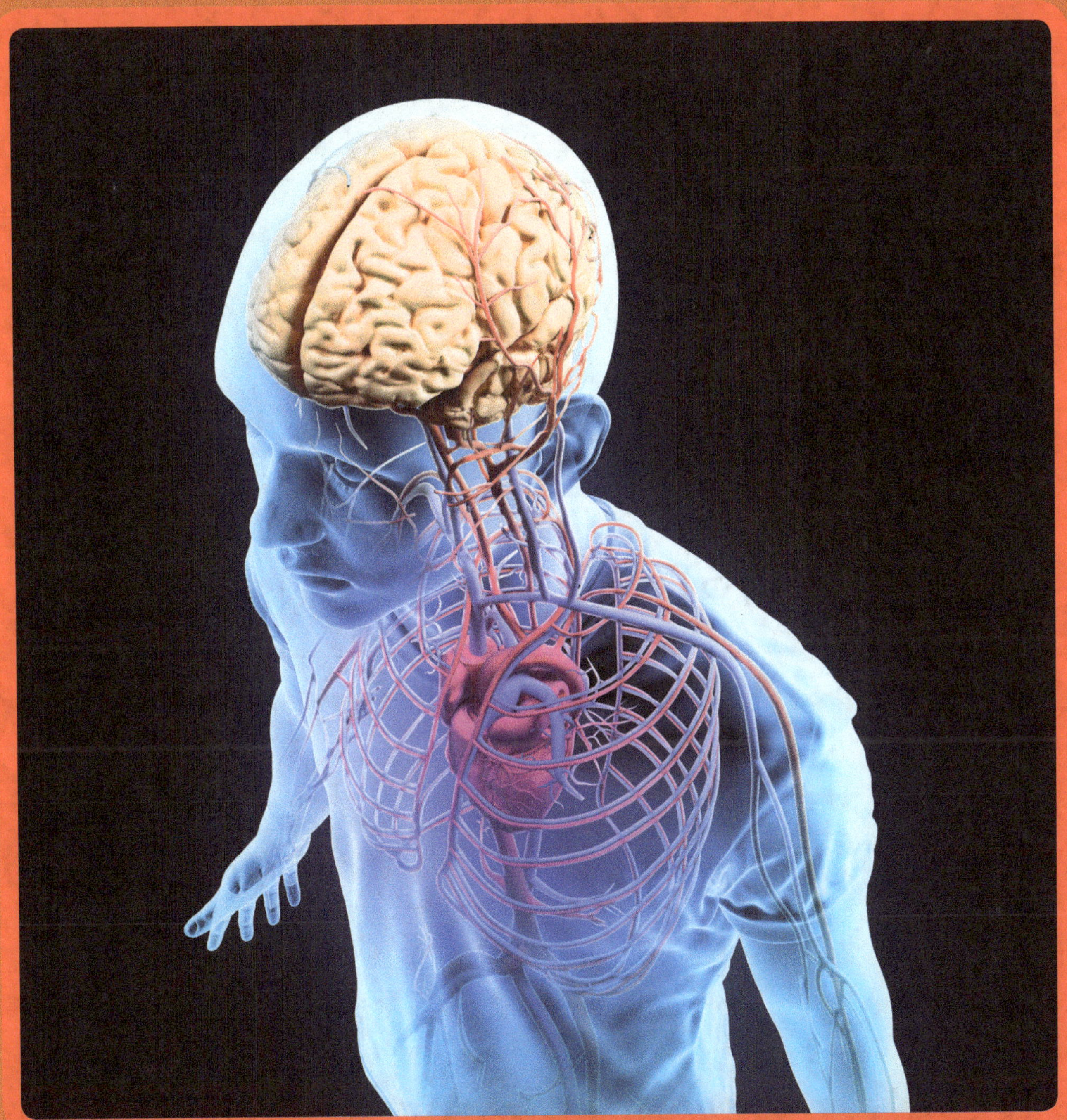

Without the nervous
system our brain
would be mush.

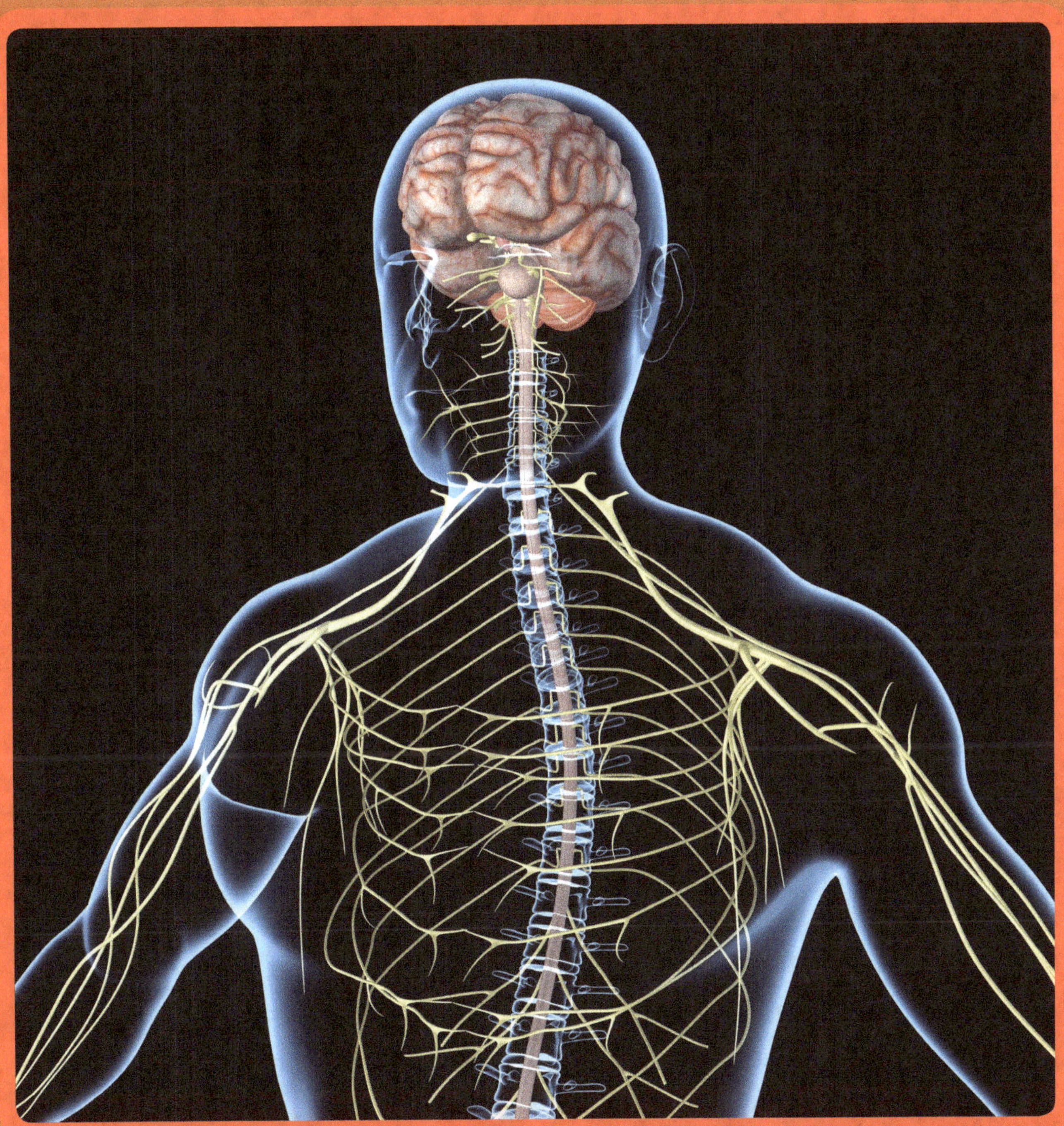

The brain and the spinal
cord make up what
is called the central
nervous system.

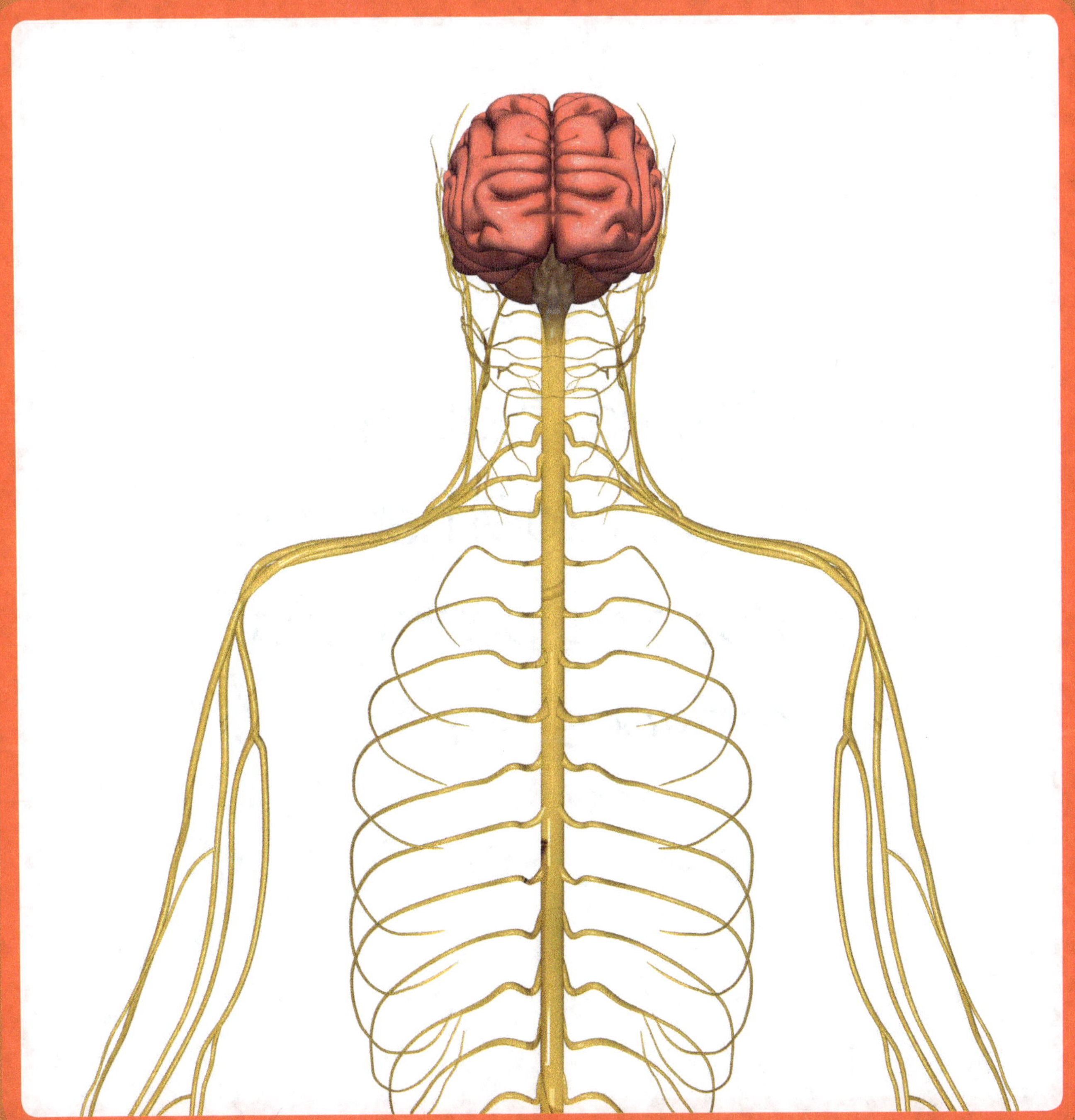

The rest of the nerves together are called the peripheral nervous system.

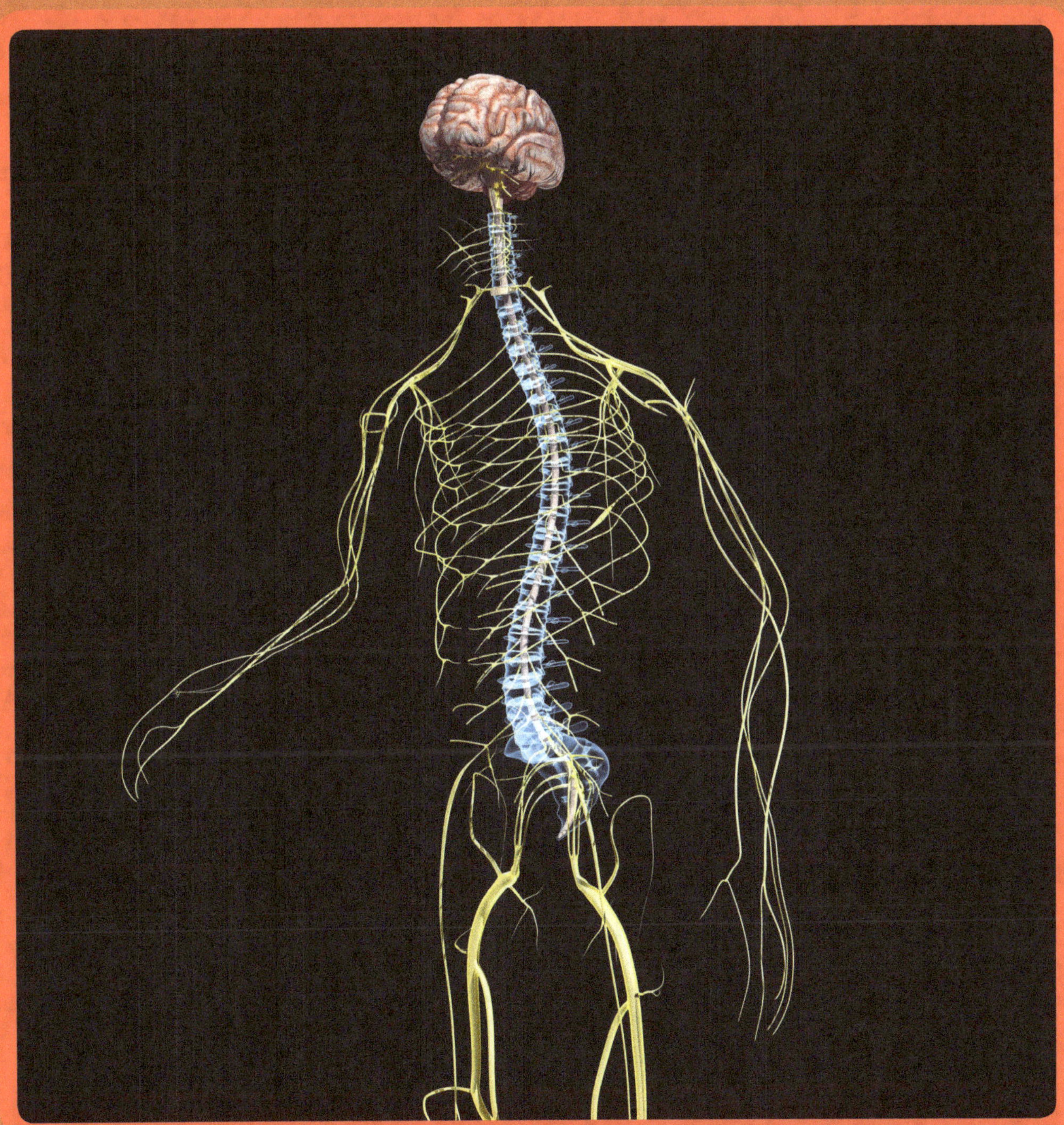

The brain is the control
centre for your body
and it sits in your
skull at the top of
your spinal cord.

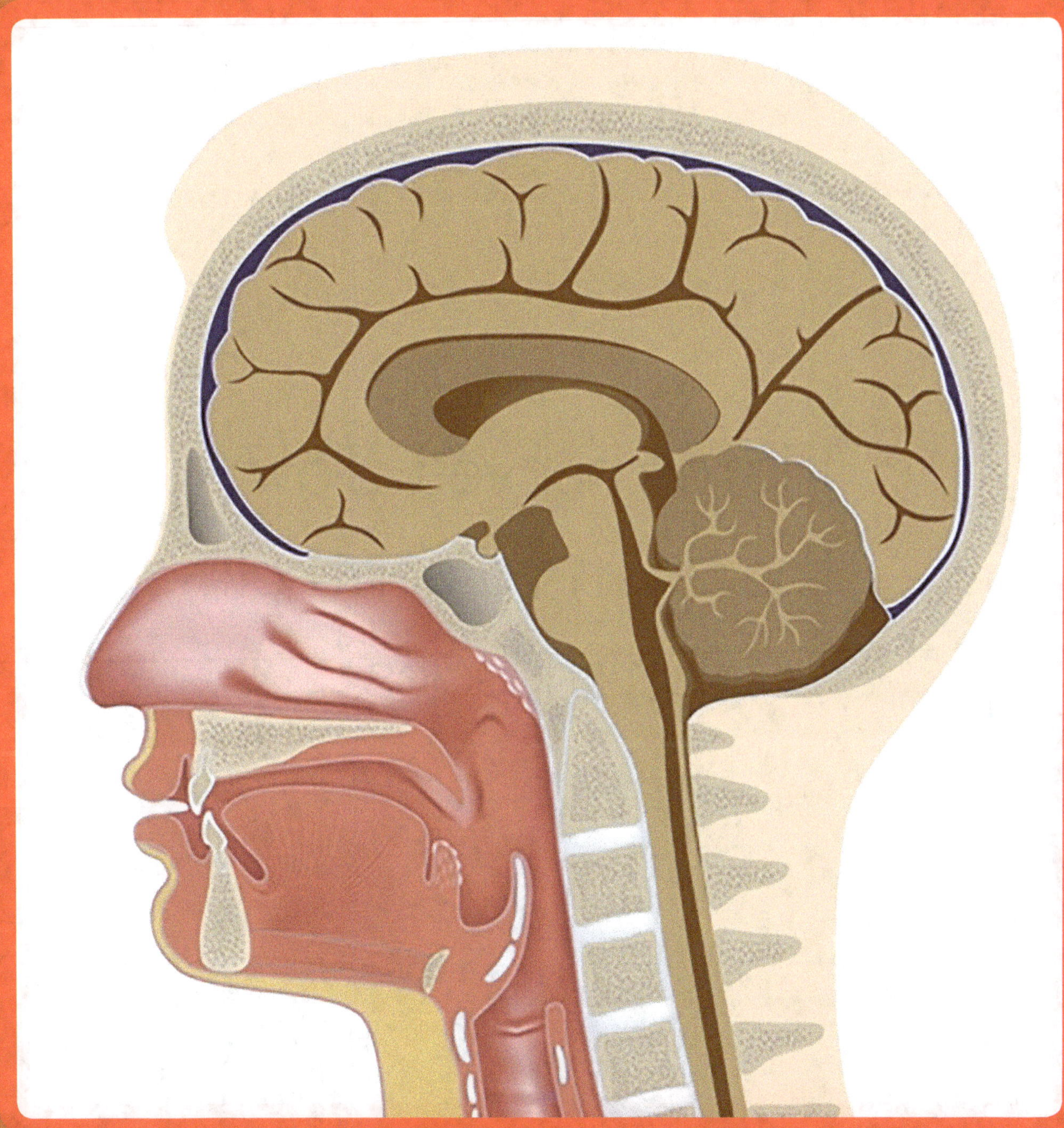

Motor nerves allow
the brain to control
our muscles.

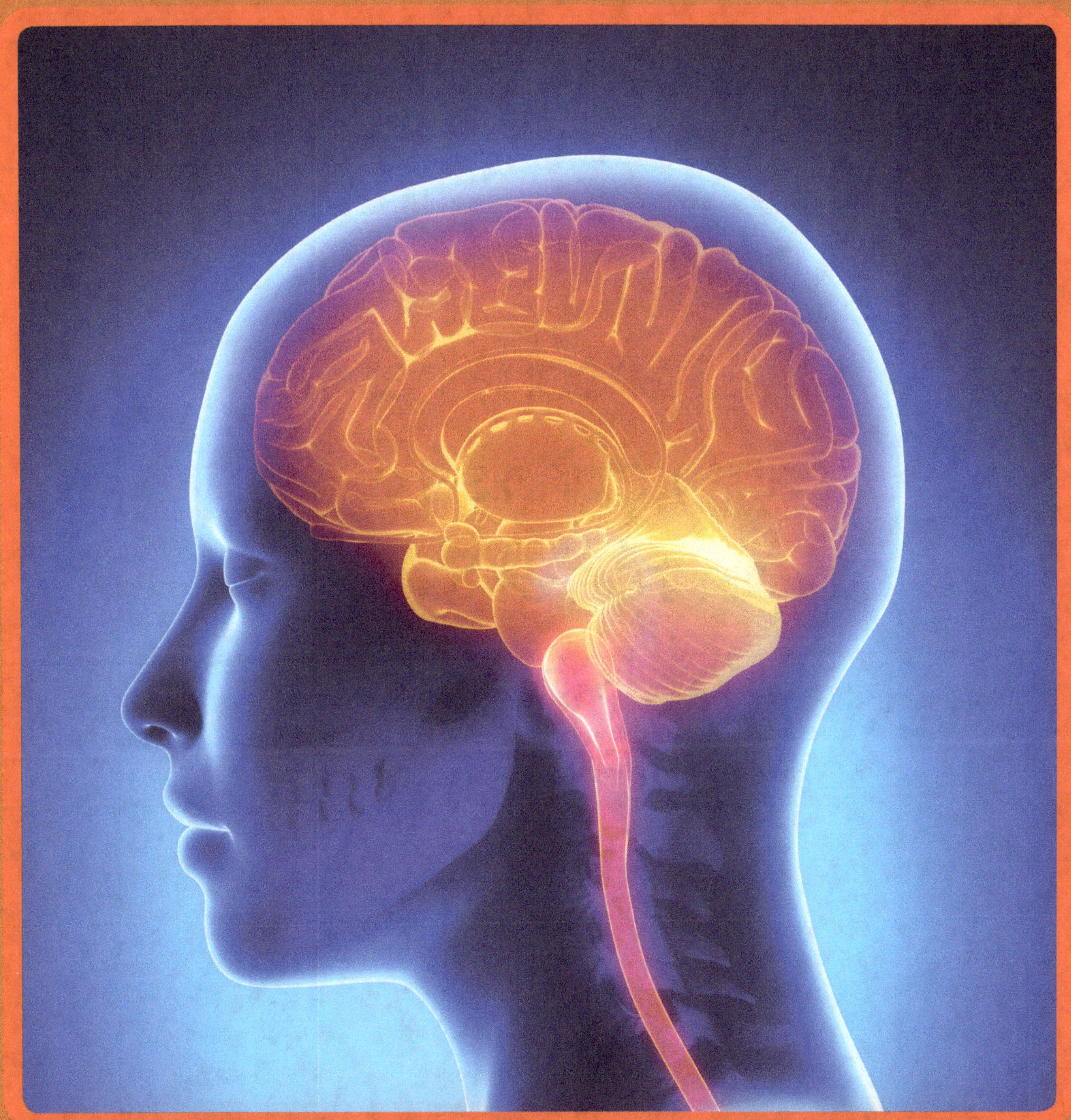

The sensory nerves carry signals to the brain to tell it about what is going on in the outside world.

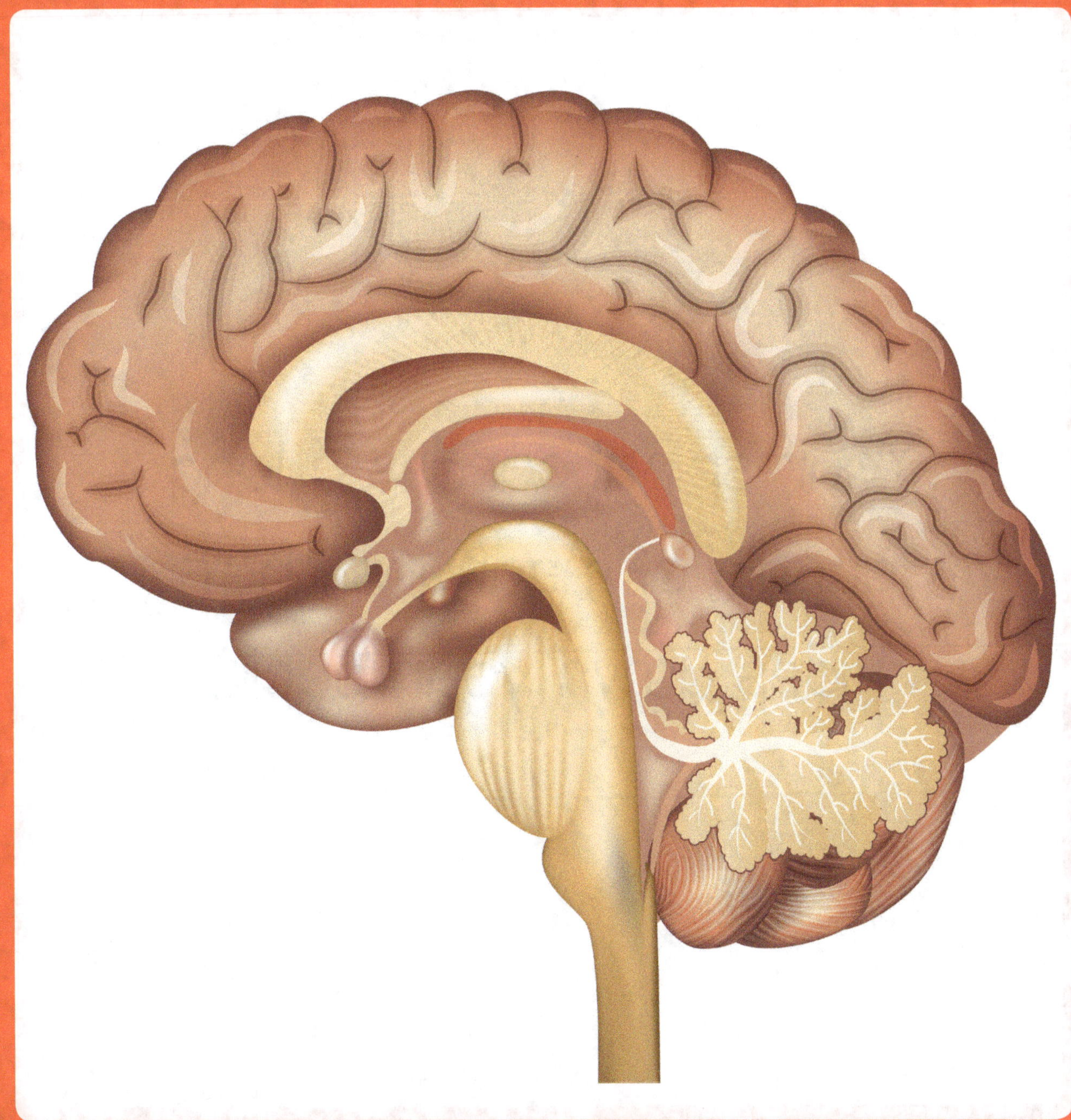

Your spinal cord is a long bundle of neurons that goes down your back.

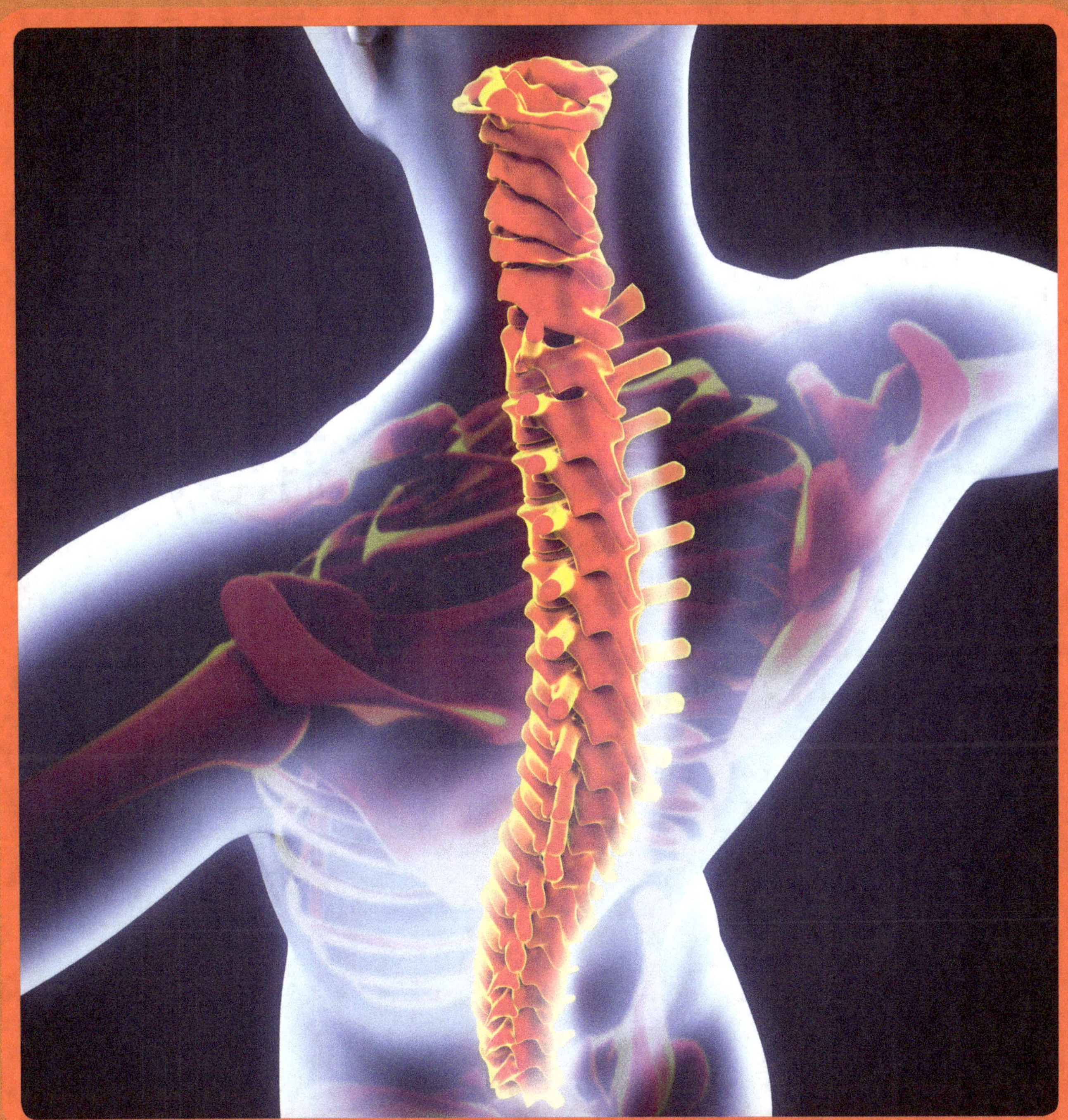

There are approximately 13.5 million neurons in the human spinal chord.

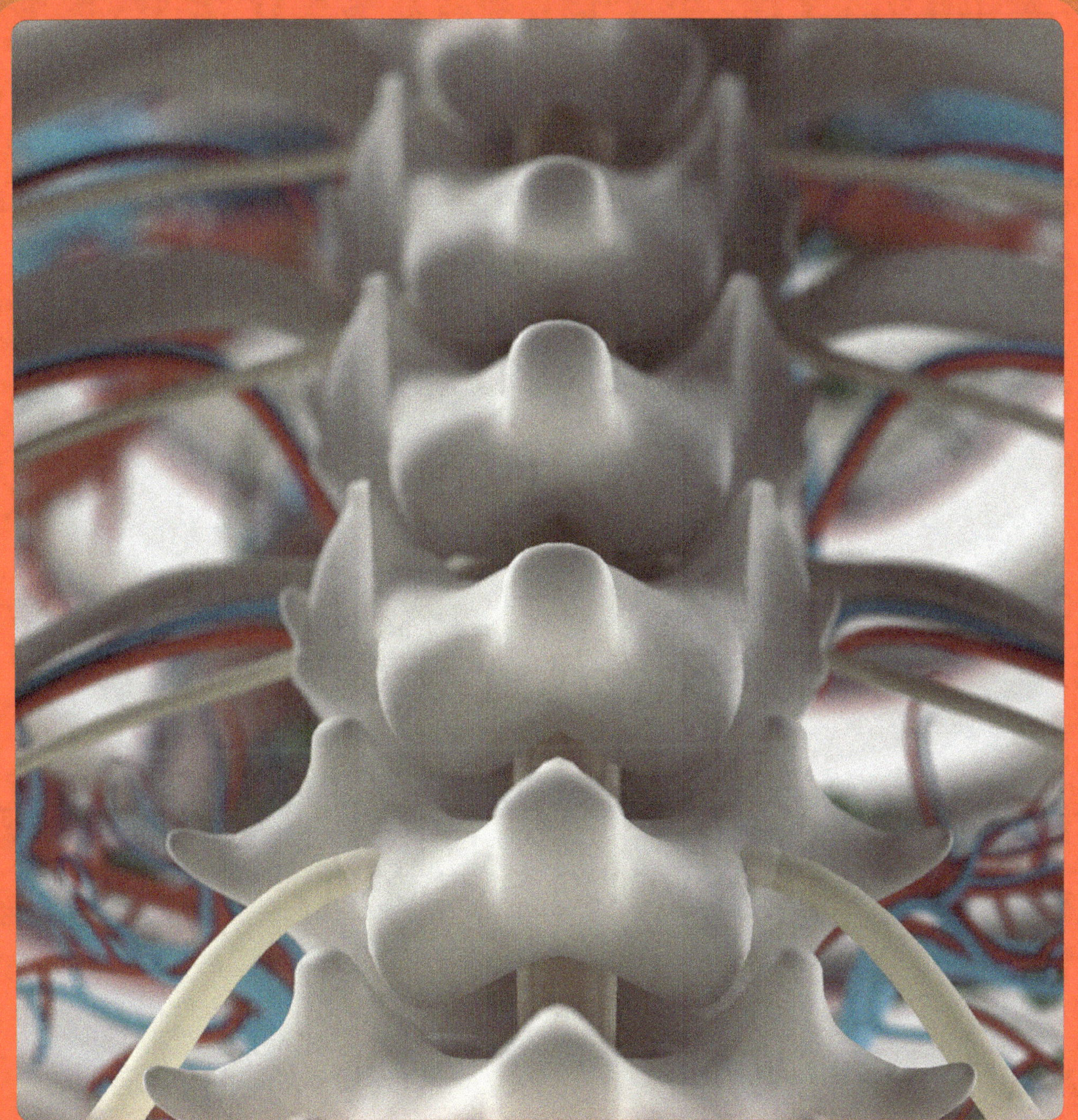

Within the peripheral nervous system there are also two main sets of nerves: the autonomic nervous system and the somatic nervous system.

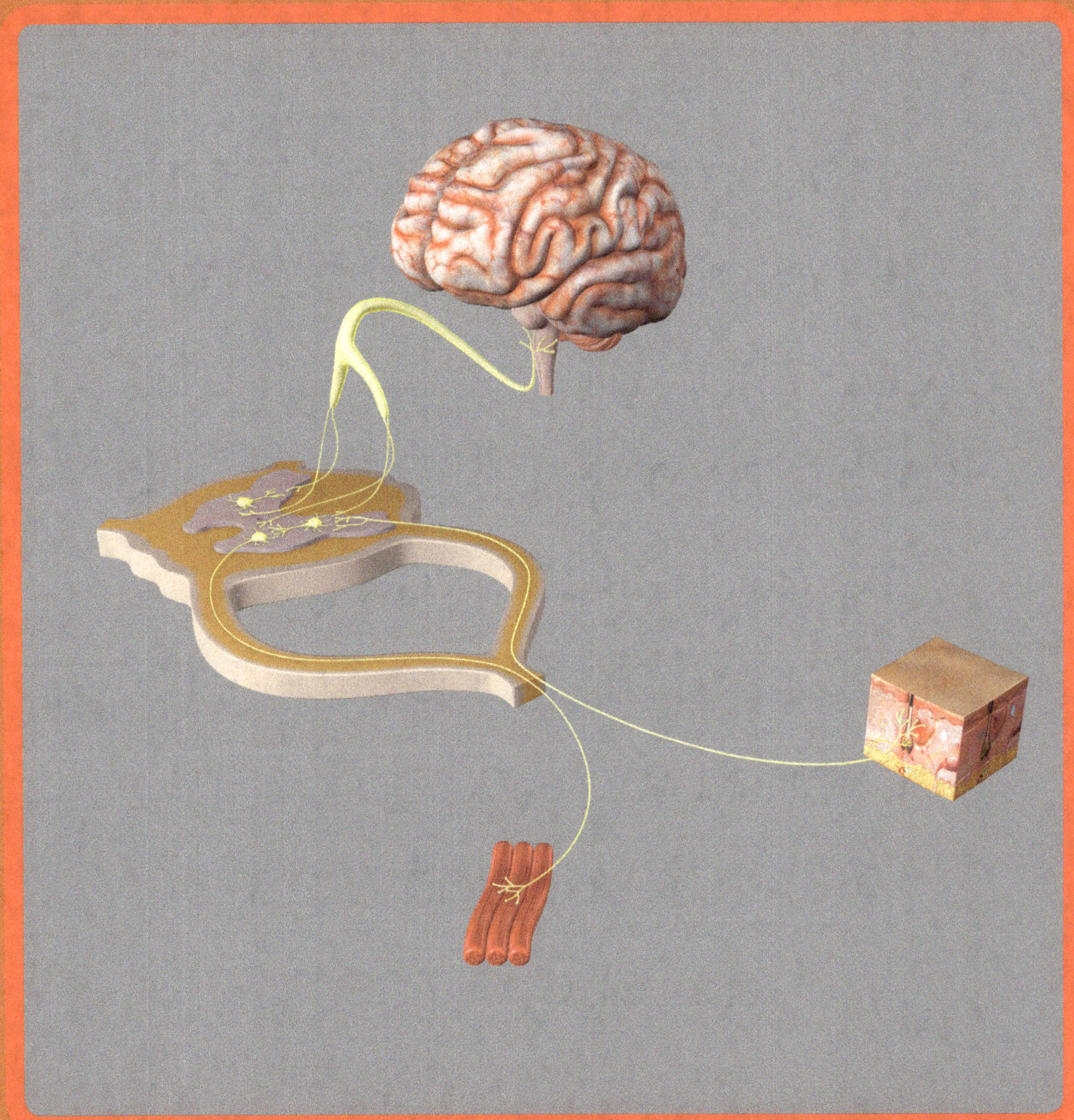

Autonomic nervous system is responsible for making sure that all the automatic things that your body needs to do to keep you going, like breathing, digesting etc continue working smoothly without your having to think about them.

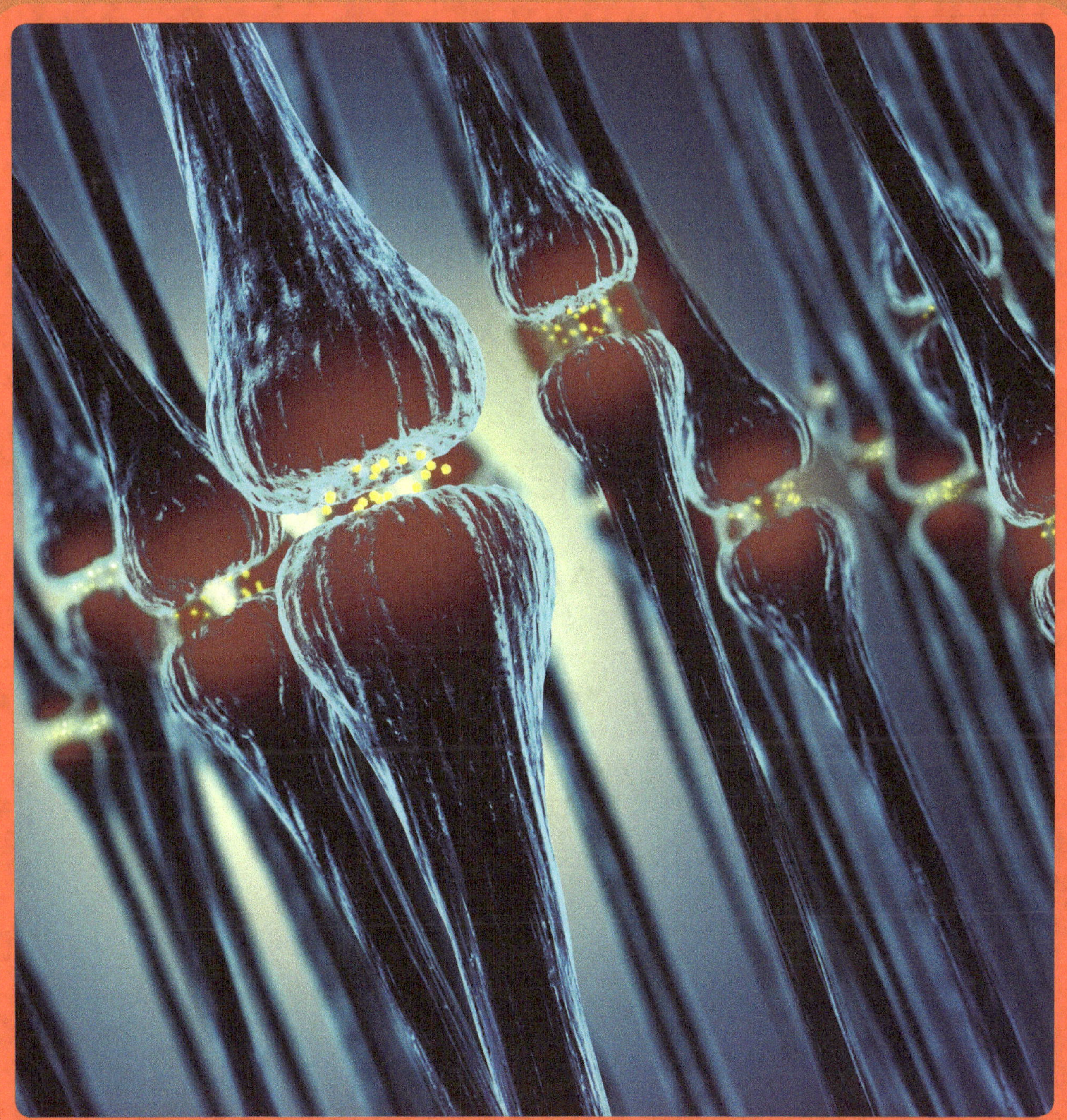

Somatic nervous system
are the nerves that
we actively control, like
jumping with our legs
or moving our arms.

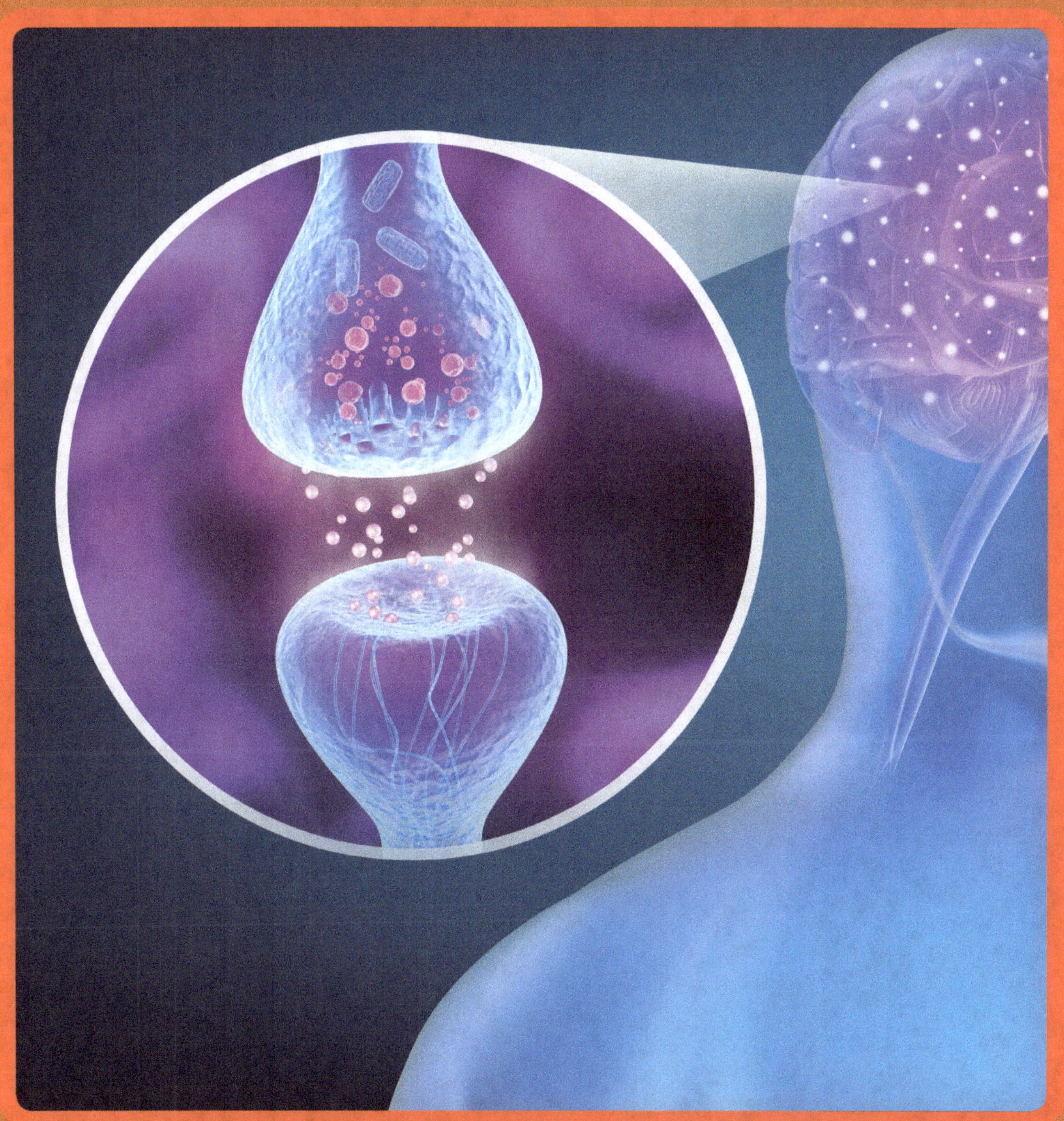

Each nerve is made
up of many cells
called neurons.

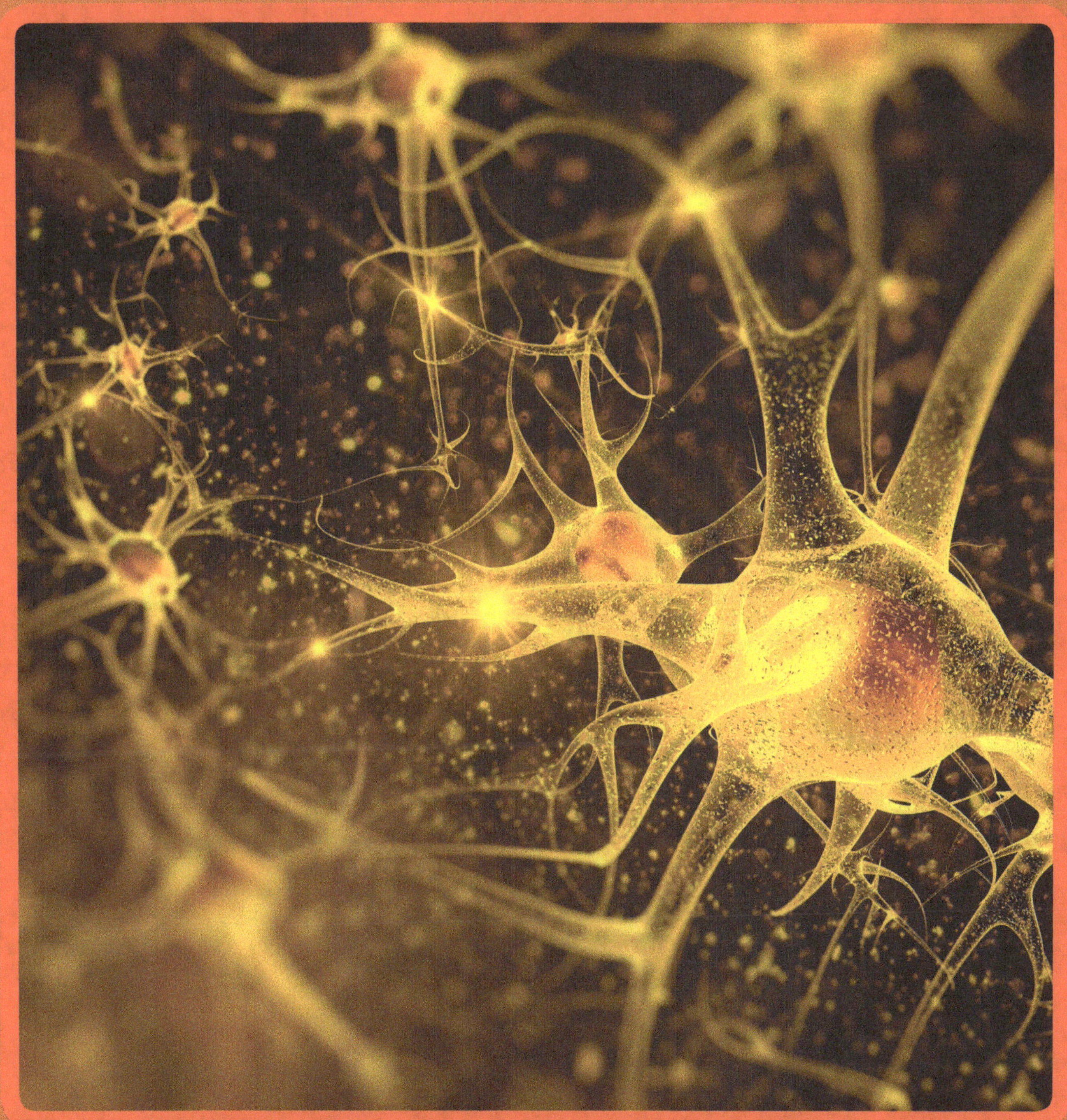

Nerves are enclosed bundles of long fibers called axons which are made up of nerve cells.

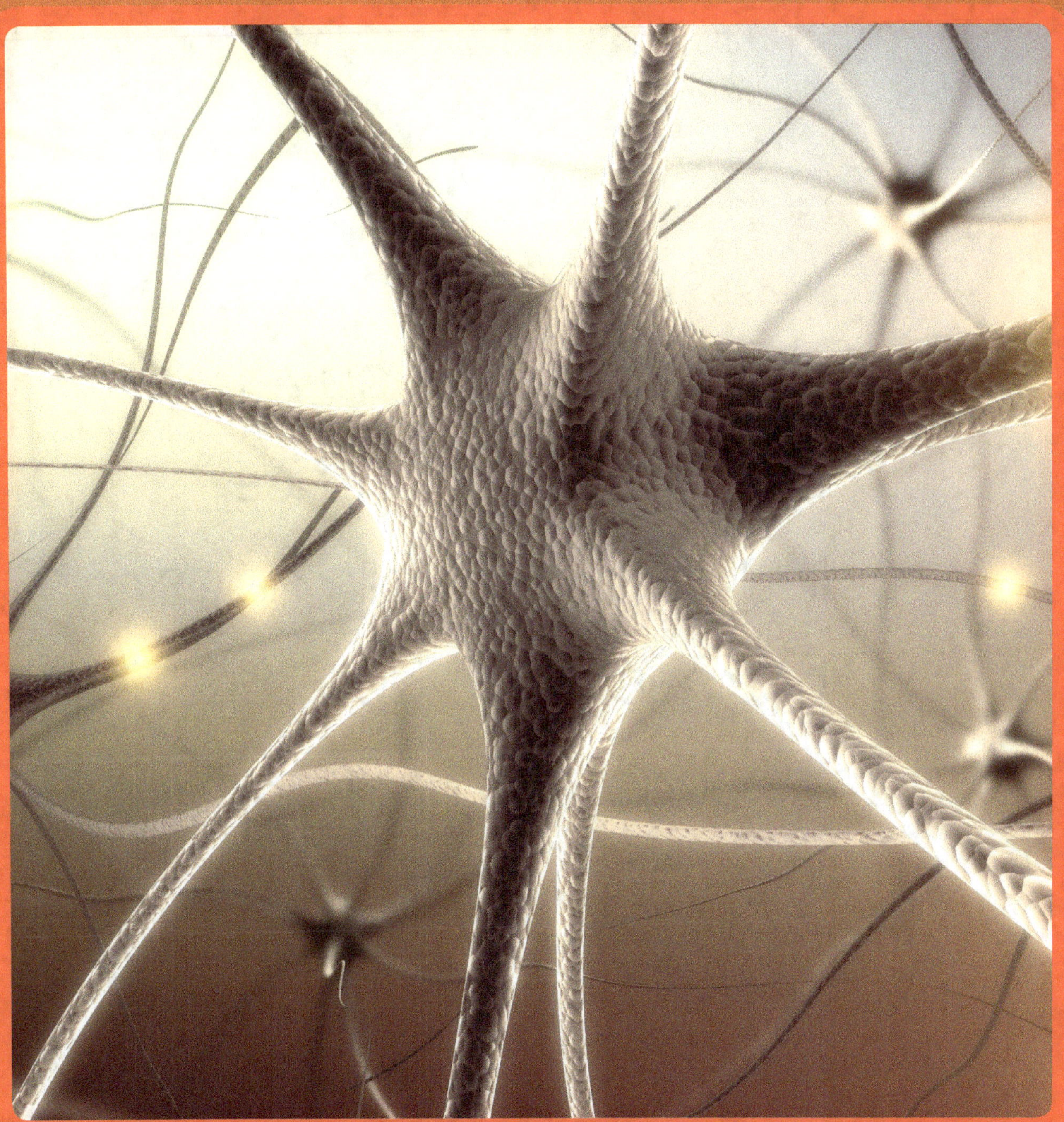

These fibres are covered by fatty substance called myelin. Myelin helps the messages go fast through the neurons.

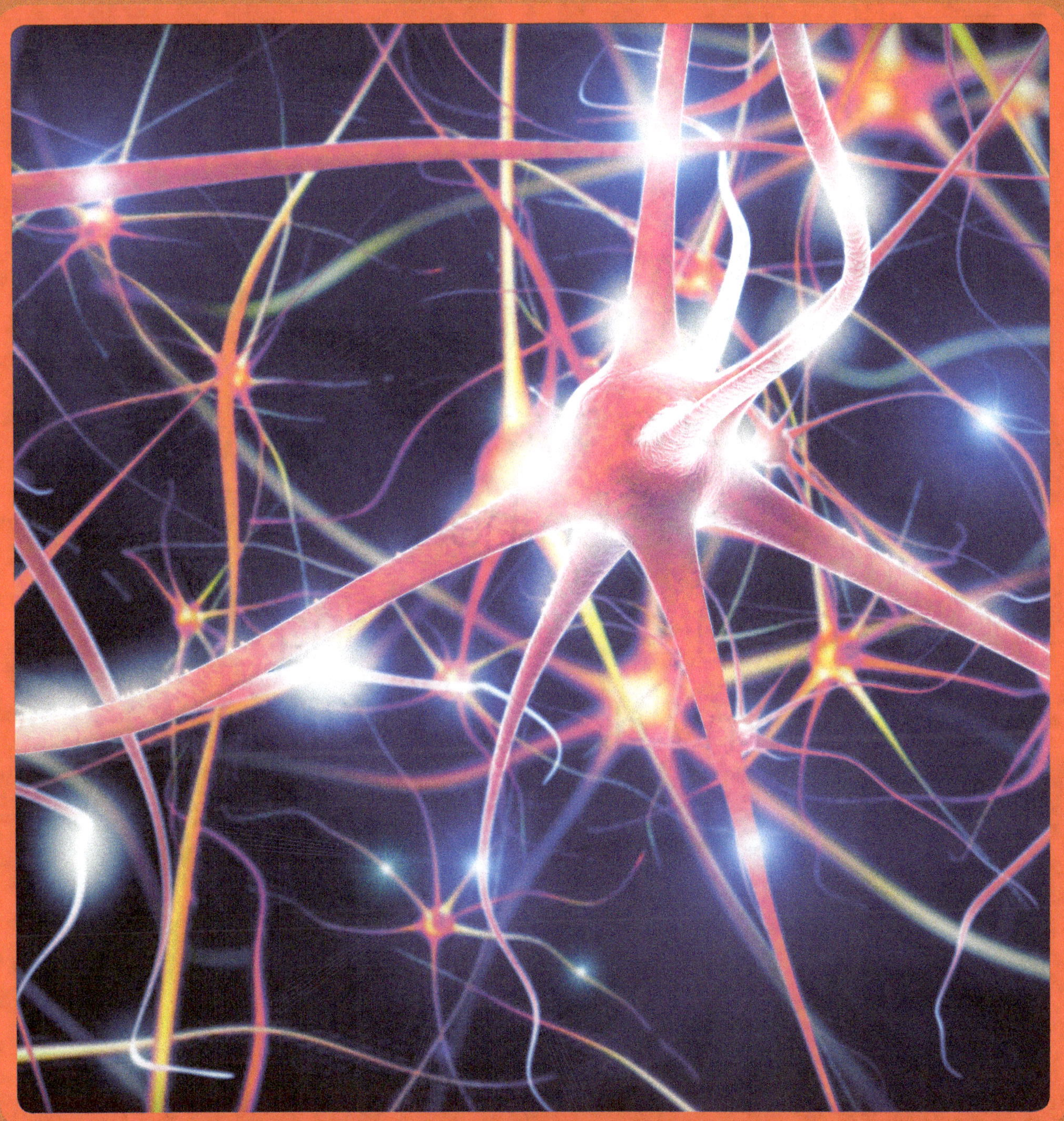

You can help your nervous system work well and be healthy by being active, having a healthy diet and keeping yourself busy and happy.

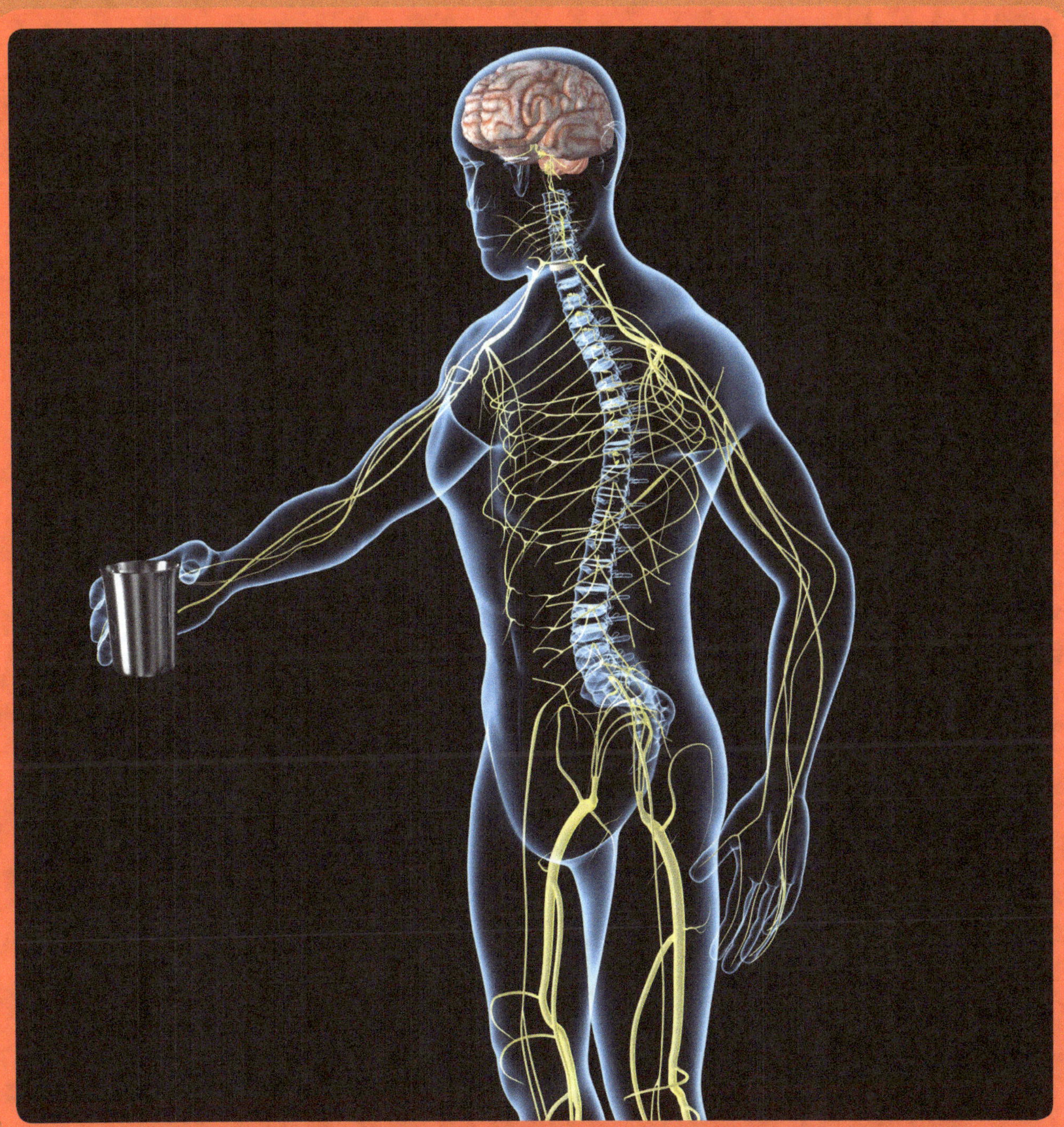

Visit
BABY PROFESSOR
EDUCATION KIDS
www.BabyProfessorBooks.com
to download Free Baby Professor eBooks
and view our catalog of new and exciting
Children's Books